The Set Table

The Art of Small Gatherings

Hannah Shuckburgh

cicada

For Archie

Contents

The Table

When I was a child, to be put in charge of setting the table was a privilege my sister and I would take in turns – it's not a job that lends itself to teamwork. To be in control of table setting was to create your own vision: to carefully count out the knives and forks – five of each – and remember which went on what side. It was to choose napkins and then match them with homemade napkin rings crafted from the inner cardboard of a loo-roll, with each person's name scrawled on the surface in felt tip. It was to fill a jug from the tap to the very, very brim and carry it – slowly, wobblingly – to the table, sloshing bits on the way. It was to remember the ketchup, the sticky bottle of squash, the huge, foot-long pepper grinder, and then to be given a small jam jar and sent into the garden to pick "only weeds, no poppies" which would form the centrepiece. At the age of 12, I mastered the paper-napkin-origami fan, inspired by one deconstructed at our local Indian restaurant, and for the next few years there was barely a supper table at home that didn't feature my handicraft.

Twenty years on, setting the table is still one of my very favourite things to do. To gather the elements of a good table: even if that is just the right plate and a proper napkin, is to set the scene. Laying a table well is to frame the food we eat, to suggest savour it, to think about style as well as content. There's nothing wrong with a snatched sandwich, standing up at a bus stop – sometimes life dictates that's how we should eat – but setting the table is about clearing away the clutter and complications of daily life, and pausing, even just for a few stolen moments.

When I go to someone's house to be greeted by a shrill hello from the kitchen, where I then see my host sweatily, franticly sieving a sauce, 17 cookbooks splayed on every surface – and I spy the kitchen table behind them, heavy with piles of bills and an open computer – I feel rather sad about the prospect of later being expected to reverently eat a soufflé or an expensive piece of beef surrounded by jus and purees and artfully placed garnishes; to feel I must grovellingly marvel at the food that has clearly been such an unmitigated headache to produce. Yes, when people are really, really hungry, they might not care whether you've filled a vase with flowers or lit candles or folded napkins, but when you're having a lovely time at someone's house, it's rarely simply because the food is nice. You will always notice when you walk into a room to find a table that has been beautifully set for you. It is a promise of good things to come.

Our kitchens are now the centre of our lives – with the kitchen table at its very heart; the place we gather for sustenance, nourishment, festivity, safety and satisfaction, but this was not always the case. The Victorians had

a very different view of dining, choosing to eat as far away as possible from the noisy, servile, messy space of the kitchen, and investing even daily family dining with enormous pomp and ceremony. In the era that saw history's largest boom in the manufacture of tableware, our dinner tables became crowded with wine glasses and napkins and all manner of specialist cutlery – from chocolate spoons to lettuce forks. Even a family of modest means would serve up to 14 dishes at a small dinner party, and each would have a new, dedicated set of cutlery. This enthusiasm for excess slowly died down in the early 20th Century, until, that is, the 1980s – fever pitch for table laying – when it became a kind of kitsch art form. It was a period of decorative floral centrepieces involving sheaves of corn and gold-painted apples, of napkin origami, basketware, flouncy tablecloths and bow-bedecked chairs. The food played second, even third fiddle to the ambitions of the table. These days, perhaps, we have gone to the other extreme. Many of us now eat standing at the kitchen counter after a long day at work, don't own any tablecloths and wouldn't dream of fussing over a floral arrangement. Our taste in glassware, crockery and china is for what is practical, washable and utilitarian. Indeed, most hip restaurants are sparse-verging-on-puritan in their placement: a bare zinc table, a white plate, a tin can stuffed with heavy steel cutlery, and a tumbler for wine – no flowers, no linens – and we have followed suit at home. Sales of napkins have plummeted and dining rooms have been consigned to National Trust stately homes.

And, for some, this might be seen as a triumph. The waning of interest in making tables look good is surely tied to the fact that women of my generation have been mostly liberated from the expectation that it is our responsibility to get a perfect meal on the table at seven o'clock sharp every evening. We, thankfully, no longer feel it is our duty to keep a perfect home – to spend our lives polishing silver or fussing over doilies. It is good news that we have long escaped that claustrophobic, degrading 1950s idea of the "perfect hostess", when newlyweds would be gifted entire, complicated sets of crockery – fondue sets and ramekins galore – which only added to the pressure. The kitchen or the dining room is no longer the site of a woman's staunchest critique, or the place which defines her; for most, it's just another room in our home.

So some might view it as a backward step to encourage an interest in crockery and cutlery when it wasn't so long ago that those were the only things women were permitted to show an interest in; but I think that is missing the point. I feel no pressure to be the perfect host, or to lay a table that looks like a fantasy from a glossy magazine, with matching cutlery, crockery and glass, polished to a gleam and costing a fortune. But making a table beautiful with scant resources gives joy – to me, to my family and to my friends. If you find it degrading, don't do it, but in this book I want to argue that investing time in a lovely table setting – just with a few simple ideas, things you can do quickly – will make the experience even more special. The food is important too, but I know few people who wouldn't prefer a simple fish pie on a lovely table – even a supper cobbled together from last-minute purchases at the corner shop (with plenty of wine and bread) over a seven-course menu that's taken you three days to produce. And I certainly don't know anyone who really loves heavily formal dinner parties, where you need to remember what fork to use and must speak to the person on your left and then your right; the ones where most of your time is spent worrying about spilling your wine or wrestling with difficult food. No, what we crave are the small, uncomplicated kinds of get-together when people's elbows touch, the type that is held amongst the pots and pans and everyday life. And it is these types of gatherings that this book is about.

On these pages I will not be encouraging you to replace all your plates and glasses, or invest in any expensive kit. I won't be bleating about measuring the millimetres between your knife and your side plate, or suggesting you make a napkin swan or start creating complex floral displays. You don't need to be brilliant at craft or cooking, or have hours of time to spare. Creating a beautiful table is not a matter of having money nor about cupboards bursting with heirloom china and priceless crystal – it's about thought and care and imagination and, mostly, generosity. I will encourage you to use and revive what you have, to make a few things yourself and to think about purpose and what feels and looks right. Set a good table, gather some friends, and everything else will fall into place.

Linens

Even a weekday lunch alone – cheese on toast and tea at the kitchen table – can be elevated with the addition of a napkin. Dinner for two on a rug on the floor of your sitting room takes on new levels of romance when a crisp tea towel is folded in half under each of your plates, and there are few more special treats than a breakfast tray set with a striped linen cloth beneath the boiled egg and soldiers. Fabrics frame a space, bring shape and tactility, blend harsh lines and offer comfort.

It was the Roman emperors who originated the idea of tablecloths – draping their banqueting tables in opulent fabrics that pooled sumptuously on the floor. The Romans were obsessed with linens. Guests at their tables

would have two napkins, one to tie round his neck, the other to wipe his fingers on. Throughout history, tablecloths have been synonymous with setting the table – a way to show wealth and generosity and to mark a meal as special. In Victorian, Edwardian and Georgian times, felt cloths were used under damask tablecloths, to guard expensive tables from heat. At traditional French dinner parties, tablecloths would be layered so that the top one could be peeled away after the first course to reveal a pristine surface for the second. Later, from the 1920s, very expensive tablecloths were replaced with placemats, doilies and runners and simple cotton coverings. In more recent decades, tablecloths have become things of practicality. Vinyl oilskin, that plastic-covered cotton printed with chintzy florals, stripes or boats, is ever more popular due to its durability and wipability. But, increasingly, we do away with tablecloths altogether and just eat on the bare wood.

Whilst tablecloths used to be things to be treasured, hand-woven or embroidered and handed down through the generations as heirlooms, their popularity over the years has plummeted. And I can understand why. Tablecloths are high maintenance. There are the issues of storage (what modern kitchen has a linen cupboard? Most of us barely have room to stack tea towels) and there's the fact you need to wash and press them after a single meal (one bad stain will ruin it). Also, if you've got a beautiful table, you may ask, why cover it? But to shake out a tablecloth over your kitchen table – a space most commonly the site of bill paying and list writing – is to announce a change of mood. Smooth the symmetrical creases of a crisply ironed tablecloth over a piece of plywood balanced on a stack of books and you set the scene. Tablecloths say: today is different. This supper is special, and you, my guests, are worth it.

Buying and making linens

Women of my generation are unlikely to acquire a bridal trousseau full of
hand-woven table linens. More often we slowly, over a lifetime, pick up our
own treasures, building a collection that is unique and distinctly our own:
Indian hand-block-printed tablecloths brought back from holidays, Victorian
lace ones rescued from junk shops, repurposed old sheets. In fact, the linens I
love most on my own table are often the cheapest ones. Brown packing paper,
cheesecloth, calico, hessian and tea towels are some of my favourite materials
for tabletops. As you are bound to have spillages of wine and wax, it seems
extravagant to lay a table with something priceless and unwashable. And
remember, a tablecloth is simply hemmed fabric bought by the metre. If you
see a fabric you like in a market or a shop, buy three metres and hem it with
iron-on tape (or don't hem it at all; fraying can look lovely on linen). Look for
a print that isn't overly complex – pale-coloured wide stripes, faded prints,
very small florals or checks in linen or cotton are best; but be sure to choose
natural fabrics – synthetics are slippery, non-absorbent, hard to clean and
stain easily. Linen is a favourite of mine – fine woven for smooth or coarsely
woven for texture. Its rugged good looks will last years and years; it washes
perfectly at a high temperature and looks beautiful even un-ironed. A length
of the cheapest white cotton (even an old sheet) or pound-per-metre calico
can be transformed into something striking and unique with a pair of scissors:
Make the prettiest, most unique cutwork tablecloth (see pictures below) by
folding a few metres of calico into panels of 10cm before chopping holes in it

Making a cut-work calico tablecloth

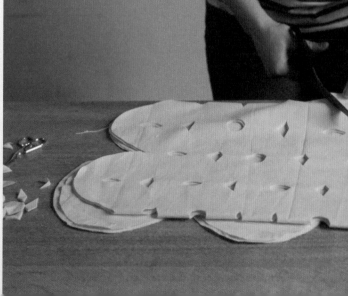

with sharp scissors (the same way you made a snowflake at nursery school) – small, centimetre-long crescents, circles and triangles a few centimetres apart. Or, tie knots in it and bind it with elastic bands and tie-dye it with Indigo dye, or paint it with bright dots using fabric paint.

For our wedding party supper, the tables were covered in raw hessian, which I bought in a huge roll from an industrial potato-sack producer and chopped to size with garden shears. Coffee sacks – particularly the ones with print and lettering on them – can make chic table-coverings, and you may be able to pick them up for free from good coffee shops. Brown packing paper (the kind you buy in the Post Office) looks simple and modern unfurled as a tablecloth with your guests' names written on it. Hammam towels – thin, often striped sarongs from West Africa – look lovely on outdoor tables; and wallpaper – if you have a roll left over – makes a good panel down the centre of a table. Victorian lace tablecloths were often made for smaller tables so are more commonly available in junk shops in round shapes. Buy them whatever size they are because lace looks beautiful with other lace – layered in a rudimentary patchwork. The unfashionable doily, too, can be found plentifully at junk shops. Collect them and sew or roughly patchwork them together to make a pretty, textured tablecloth. If you find an embroidered or drawn-threadwork antique tablecloth that's too small for your table, lay a piece of plain cotton under it, so the old one is a centrepiece. Remember, on a good table, things don't fit exactly.

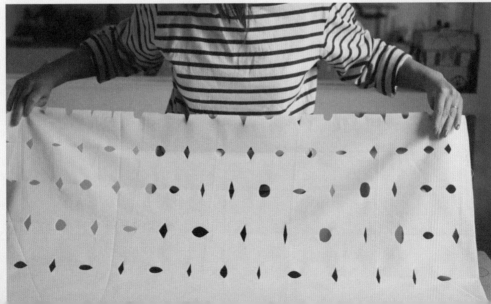

Some types of tablecloth

French printed
Modern French markets are filled
with great rolls of vibrantly printed,
garish cloth – yellow and blue,
mostly, and featuring farmhouse
motifs. French-style tablecloths with
wide, colourful stripes are lovely for
summer lunches outdoors.

Lace
Deeply feminine and very special,
traditional lace is handwoven and
expensive. It looks lovely even when
ancient and frayed, and matches wild
flowers and chipped china perfectly.

Damask
Originally from Damascus, in Syria, Damask
has always been synonymous with the grandest
tables. It used to be highly patterned, reversible
woven silk with embroidery. These days it's
more likely to be a mix of silk, linen, wool
and other synthetics, but it's still heavy,
expensive and requires lots of attention.
It must be professionally cleaned and pressed
after a single use.

Drawn threadwork
Popular on Edwardian and Victorian tables, these pretty whitework tablecloths involve 'counted thread' weaving, whereby single threads are removed to create beautiful patterns. Even a small cloth will look very special on a coffee tray.

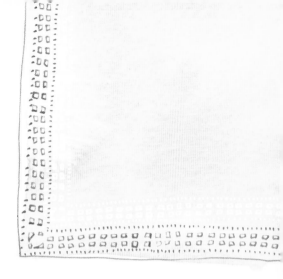

Indian hand-block-print
Often printed with vegetable dyes, these fabrics fade beautifully over time and are ideal for candlelit dinners on urban roof terraces. Look for tight, small prints – they make lovely napkins too.

Vinyl-coated oilskin
A wipeable, plastic-coated cotton that is popular in nursery schools and family kitchens.

Checked
Synonymous with Mediterranean trattorias and tavernas, red-and-white checked cotton is easy to clean and forgiving of stains. Looks good on breakfast tables.

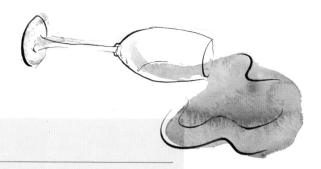

How to get stains out of tablecloths

Contrary to what you've heard, no amount of salt, stain remover or white wine will remove red wine spilt on a white cloth. There is only one way to get it out, and that is with cold, cold water, and plenty of it. With any stain – oil, wine, tomato – you need to flood it with cold water immediately, and I mean drench it. Hot water will set a stain and soap will only give you the illusion you are washing it out. As soon as a stain dries, you are unlikely to be able to shift it, so act quickly with a jug-full of water. With smaller stains, eye makeup remover is incredibly effective, as are baby wipes. Keep some under your sink and use on your clothes too, for spot-cleaning.

Napkins

If the tablecloth is in decline, the napkin is positively endangered. In a recent survey it was revealed that only 15 per cent of us lay the table with napkins. Such a shame, because I love a good napkin. People say they are pointless, but where do you wipe your fingers? How do you mop your chin when you've been eating buttery artichokes? Really, a piece of flimsy kitchen roll just isn't the same, is it?

It wasn't until the early 19th Century that napkins moved from being tied around the neck to being draped over knees. Personally, I love the look

of a napkin tucked into a shirt collar – especially with food you eat with your hands, like lobster. Until recently, tucking your napkin into your shirt was a sign of incivility – but I think, nowadays, it looks like you're hungry and mean business about eating; a good thing at any table. I am always really uncomfortable at a table without a napkin. I find myself searching for it on my lap, wiping my hands on my dress. I want supersize. The bigger the better. A small tablecloth I can shake out with a flourish and cover my lap with, not some pocket-sized square that would barely suffice as a handkerchief. A good napkin should cover your knees even when folded in half.

Very few of my own napkins match. There are the soft, almost threadbare ones that belonged to my grandmother, block-printed ones, linen ones in different colours that have been washed a thousand times, and a few purloined from restaurants. You don't need a whole set, and napkins are not expensive, but why not make some yourself? Arm yourself with iron-on hemming tape (or use a sewing machine, of course) and it could not be easier. Allow 50cm square – I know that sounds huge, but you'll need it – and

then hem the four edges. Look for interesting patterns and materials in the remnant bins in fabric shops. French dishcloths (for sale in all supermarkets there) make brilliant napkins: big, soft and washable. The vintage ones, if you can find them, are the gold standard for napkin lovers like me – in particular the old white napkins with embroidered initials (it doesn't matter if they're not your own). Hunt them down and cobble together a mismatched set.

We associate the trend for napkin origami – starch-sprayed and contorted into lotus flowers, swans, fans and dinner jackets – with the 1980s, but in fact, we have been obsessing over the fold of our napkins since the 16th Century. Napkin art reached its zenith in 17th Century Versailles, where *serviettes* were folded into frogs, boats, even chickens sitting on eggs. These intricate constructions, crafted by people for whom napkin wrangling was not just an art but a profession, were not even designed to be used. Another napkin would be provided for the purposes of actual sticky fingers. On my table, however, I like to see a napkin that looks ready to use – a simple roll or gentle fold, either on top of the plate, or to the side; under the knife or with both the knife and fork resting on top. I don't use napkin rings myself, but I like the idea of a little tie of string, some ribbon or a little foliage for a special supper. Don't hide things (like bread) in your napkin as they are most likely to roll out and end up on the floor.

Placemats

The laminated placemats printed with rural scenes or architectural gems so beloved in the 1980s are never going to look stylish, and I wouldn't want anything plastic under a plate. Placemats, by and large, are excessive on most tables, I think, unless they are for very hot dishes from the oven. Trivets for pans or pots should be sturdy: slate, wood off-cuts and wrought iron. But for the plates themselves, I rarely use a placemat underlay. Dinner plates should never be so hot they risk scalding the table, and a matching set of placemats that serve no purpose can look very bland. But on some occasions, a little fabric or texture under each place can look lovely, especially at very small gatherings: supper for two in front of the fire, say. Rough textures are best because plates won't slip and slide: try a folded striped tea towel, a rectangle of hessian or a circle of woven straw.

Crockery

I dream of whiling away my twilight years in a cottage with a dresser groaning under the weight of jugs and mugs and plates and bowls gathered over a lifetime. The best crockery collections are built up slowly: the salt cellar from a tourist shop in Sicily; the spongeware bowl from Ireland; mugs from museum shops; and endless jugs from rural antique shops and charity shops. Ceramics and pottery bring shape and contrast to the table, but they can also allow you to play with the notes of your food. Studies have shown that strawberries taste sweeter against white and more sour against blue. And nobody needs to be told that tea tastes better drunk out of china than from Styrofoam. What we put food in and on has a transformative effect.

On her wedding day, my grandmother was given a complete set of china. From soup tureens to milk jugs, side plates and cereal bowls, she was set for life against a background of blue and white Wedgewood. To my generation, the idea that we would have to choose one pattern of plate to live with for our whole life would be impossible. The 'dinner service' has died a death. We're unlikely to start married lives, or indeed any new chapter, with a blank slate, not owning a single plate or pan or spoon, and so, more often than not, our kitchens are a cluttered patchwork of things we have picked up along the way. Our crockery cupboards are a testament to how interesting our lives have been; the chapters that have come before, the places we've seen, the kitchens and suppers we've known. One matching set of Royal Doulton would not express that history, and so it is right and natural that our crockery collections should be built, rather than bought.

Big, cheap, clean white plates are endlessly replaceable, always look right and arguably are best for eating off as they never clash with the food, but painted plates are decorative and collectable and will bring colour and character to the table. When I open the door of my crockery cupboard – precariously stacked with mismatched plates and bowls and jugs – I don't want to be met with a sea of boring white. I want cupboards bursting with every shape and size, print and colour: small, striped jugs for the coffee tray; large, flat, emerald plates for summer salads; floral jugs for double cream; glass pots for mayonnaise; wooden coupes for winter porridge. There is no better place to score the odds and ends of your crockery cupboard than your local charity shop.

Buying crockery second-hand

Gone are the days when you might find an Ossie Clark dress in the 10p bin
of your local thrift store, but ceramics, pottery and tableware are a massive
untapped resource. I know it's annoying to be told you can pick things up in
charity shops – when for most of us there is nothing there but moth-eaten
jumpers and games of Monopoly with missing pieces – but if you are not
searching for priceless antiques, you will be able to stock your cupboards
amply with beautiful and distinctive crockery.

There is a skill to rationalising the wares on a bric-a-brac shelf. On a
crowded shelf of mawkish figurines and scratched CDs, you must try to see

each bowl or jug as an individual. Pick every crockery item up, look at it and imagine it out of context – in a chic interiors shops, say, or on a table in the garden, full of sweet peas. Things which look tatty and unloved in a junk shop might look completely charming styled well. Stand back and squint. Remember, it's not what it's worth, it's what it's worth to you.

When collecting second-hand crockery, it's good to have a theme to stick to. Perhaps it might be roses, sherbet colours or all the shades of green. Having a theme will make it easy to pinpoint things in and amongst the rubble.

Turn crockery over and look at the base. By understanding the names and symbols printed on the back, you can get a sense of its origin and, occasionally, its value. The great pottery companies will promise the best quality – look for Spode, Royal Worcester, Poole, Royal Doulton, Denby, Wedgwood and Crown Derby. Now examine the mark – is it cut into the clay or is it painted or printed on? Incised or handpainted marks indicate an earlier piece. A printed mark usually implies that the piece is 19th Century or later. An image of Royal Arms, the words 'Limited', 'Ltd' or 'Trade Mark' all indicate that the piece was made after 1862. The words 'England', 'Bone China' or 'Royal' are more common in 20th Century pieces.

Much of the crockery in charity shops is likely to be 1980s reissues of traditional designs. Descriptions of the piece such as 'Genuine Staffordshire Ware' or 'Ye Olde Willow' are indications that this is likely. Look at the colour of the piece – originals tend to be darker. Then, run your hand over the print. Older, hand-painted items won't have a protective glaze, so will have a slightly raised pattern, whilst later, glazed pieces will be completely smooth to the touch. Look for chips, cracks and signs of repair, and then put the plate on a solid surface and check is sits flat (some older plates will wobble).

Types of crockery

Rustic and everyday

Pottery is clay fired at a low temperature, so it is quite porous. It's lovely for dry things, like salt or even cherries, but it can be tricky as a vase as it will absorb and then leach out water. Pottery is thick, heavy and easily chipped, but is often artisanal and one-off. Studio pottery – pieces handmade by potters – can be expensive, as they are collectable, and were often designed to be works of art, rather than for practical use. I have a few pieces of homemade pottery picked up in junk shops that may well be by children for all I know, but I love their freeform shape and haphazard painted surfaces. Don't be put off by imperfections in pottery – it all adds character.

Earthenware is similar to pottery in that it feels thick and rustic, but it is vitrified and glazed so it is opaque, dense and more durable. As it's fired at low temperatures it can be made in strong, bright colours – rich red and green, for example. *Stoneware* is even more dense than earthenware – it's affordable and hardwearing and is what most of our daily crockery is made of.

Painted plates

Spongeware is crockery that has been hand-painted with ink-dipped sponge moulds. The most collectable, antique pieces were made between the 1830s and the 1930s, but modern potteries, like Nicholas Mosse, Bell Pottery, Emma Bridgewater and Brixton Pottery make beautiful pieces that are affordable and easy to collect. It has a homespun, country-kitchen feel. *Cornish Blue*, the distinctive, wide blue-and-white striped crockery, was made by T E Green in Derbyshire, and is still being produced – a Cornish Blue jug begs to be filled with custard. Italian and other Meditteranean painted pottery is distinguished by its brightly coloured, busy patterns.

Fine and special

Porcelain is fine and fragile, made from a combination of clays – kaolin, quartz and feldspar – fired at a very high temperature to make it extremely hard. It is non-porous, smooth and prettily semi-transluscent. If you hold a porcelain plate to the light and pass your hand behind it, you'll see its shadow. The best porcelain pieces are by Rosenthal, Lenox, Noritake and pieces made in the porcelain Mecca of Limoges in France. *Bone china* is a type of porcelain that contains ash (usually animal bone) is a very pale, creamy white (most porcelain is grey-ish) and light – almost see-through.

For the best fine china, look to Wedgewood, Royal Crown Derby, Royal Doulton, Minton and Spode. Many of the most beautiful fine china pieces will be made by British factories that have since, sadly, gone bust. For these deadstock pieces, look for Bow, Chelsea, Longton Hall, Bristol, Coalport and Rockingham. From the continent, Sevres from France and Meissen from Germany are treasures.

Other types

Melamime, a tough, nearly indestructible, treated plastic that can be brightly coloured and cheaply produced, became popular in the USA in the 1930s – when women wanted kitchens that were modern and practical. Melamime, like other plastic plates, stands up to repeat washing and is perfect for picnics. It looks best when its kitcshness is played up – a Melamime platter for a sherbet-coloured iced birthday cake, say, or a Melamime bowl for a heap of toffee popcorn. Plastic plates can look fun when the colours clash, so don't get a set. For really collectable pieces, look for Russell Wright, Branchell, American Cyanide, Flair, Fortiflex and Color-Flyte.

Enamelware is made of porcelain and steel – most famously by Falcon, the maker of the classic white-with-blue-rim cups we took camping as children. It has the holy trinity of being cheap, practical and beautiful: perfect for daily use.

Tin, which can bring to mind the image of prison inmates clattering their plates against their bars, has, like many things from humble origins, soared in popularity. You can still buy tin cups and serving plates at camping shops, but don't relegate them to the lower eschelons of dining. Chipped tin – the really old pieces which look almost speckled, looks especially good when used in contrast – a vase for some elegant roses; or a tin platter for a rare beef fillet.

Shapes and sizes

Plate shapes

In the 1990s, it seemed dinner plates would take over the table. In restaurants, as the food got smaller, the plates got larger. Huge great squares and rectangles made even the most generous supper look a little mean, and threatened to oust the humble round plate for good. But, happily, the round plate is back. Every size of plate has a use, from dinky cake plates to generous platters for roasts, and a well set table will have a nice mix of sizes – little dishes for salt, and large plates for salads. But for serving the main course at lunch or supper, keep your guests' plates a similar size for uniformity and fairness of portion size. I think the best size for a main course is a lunch plate (see right) – it's chic and compact and makes food look generous – but for real feasting (like at Christmas), I want a huge plate (even a charger) that has space for everything in one helping.

Charger
Oversized dinner plates – sometimes 30cm in diameter – are designed to be place plates. They 'hold' the place setting, so the table doesn't look too empty. They're removed when plates with actual food on them arrive. Really the preserve of restaurants, rather than gatherings at home.

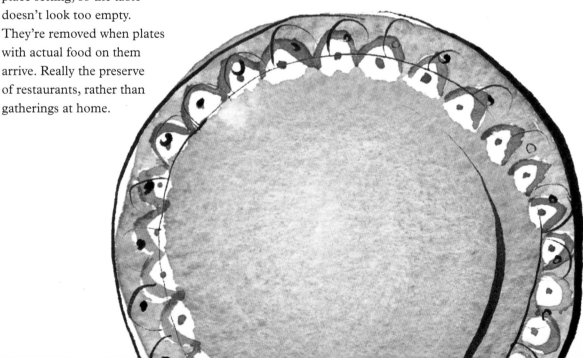

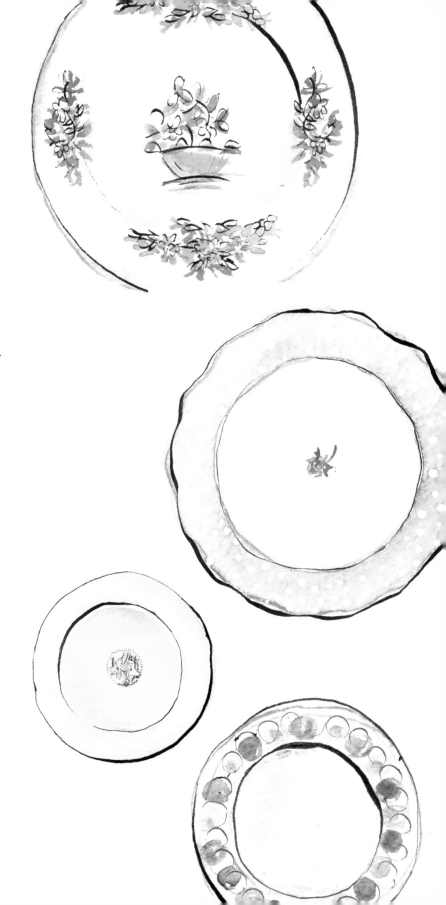

Dinner plate
The classic size for a dinner plate is round, rimmed and about 28cm in diameter. Designed to fit meat and three veg comfortably.

Lunch plate
A lunch plate is slightly smaller – 26cm in diameter and just the right size for a few slices of cold ham and salad.

Side plate
A classic side plate – on grand tables placed to the left, above or to the side of the forks – is for bread and is normally about 18cm in diameter.

Pudding plate
Normally 20cm in diameter, these were intended to serve solid puddings like tarts, or for cakes at teatime.

Bowl Shapes

The benefit of a nice bowl is that it will make servings look generous. Bowls are either rimmed or coupe-shaped, but their use is dictated by their depth: deep for cereal, shallow for thin soups and bouillon. Thick and hearty recipes call for deep, thick, chunky bowls; delicate puddings in small portions – lemon posset or chocolate mousse – call for low, slim and shallow.

Cream soup cup and stand
A footed bowl with two
handles, which sits on a little
saucer, designed for soup.
They can make lovely low
bowls for flowers.

Rimmed Soup bowl
Soup bowls are shallow and
wide, and, if rimmed, are
about 23cm in diameter.

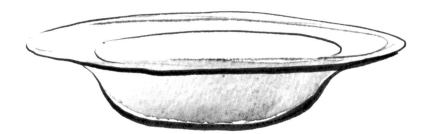

Coupe cereal bowl
Cereal and porridge bowls
need depth. Typically with
a diameter of 18cm.

Fruit or pudding bowl
A small version of a cereal
bowl – 16cm or so in
diameter – designed for soupy
puddings, like rhubarb and
custard.

Serving platters

Unless you run your kitchen like a restaurant, where each guest's plate is constructed in a production line – arranged in a row on the counter to be anointed with a smear of jus and an accurate placement of garnish – you will be bringing your cooking to the table for your loved ones to help themselves. Doling out regimented portions can seem mean and controlling, whereas bringing it to the table feels more generous, and allows people to be choosy – or to eat not very much if they want to. I love carving up a big joint of roasted meat, and bringing it on a huge platter so that my guests can pick the bits they like. When you serve things off-stage, even if you ask people how much they want, you're drawing too much attention to how hungry (or greedy) they are. Just let it happen.

In our grandparents' generation, hostesses would not have dared bring a charred-edged cooking pan to the table, still steaming and greasy from the hob, preferring instead to decant each dish into a sterile, lidded platter that matched their crockery set. But nowadays, it would seem mad to create more washing up, and really, nothing is more mouth-watering than something that has clearly come from the oven. So serve food straight from the kitchen, in the vessels you used to cook it. Double handled pots – like the cast-iron, heavy-bottomed casseroles by Staub, Emile Henry and Le Creuset – look instantly revived when a clean linen tea towel is wrapped round the handles. Cast iron has been used for hundreds of years for cooking – so heavy and durable it can be put straight on a fire. Season yours regularly with oil to keep it non-stick and rust free; clean it with sea salt massaged in with kitchen towel.

Casserole dishes in materials that conduct heat can look beautiful – terracotta dishes, enamelware trays or Morroccan tagines, or, for a plainer look, glass and china. Miniature oven-to-tableware is also cute; I love two fried eggs brought to the breakfast table still in their mini saucepan.

But serving platters really come into their own when presenting side dishes. Peas in a saucepan look like an afterthought, but tip them into a warmed dish – maybe a clashing green earthenware one – and, tossed with lots of butter and torn shreds of mint – they take centre stage. A simple roast chicken looks like a feast when it is accompanied by a wide, flat, faded-painted platter arranged with thinly sliced tomatoes scattered with

sea salt, and a fat, wooden bowl of steaming new potatoes. Serving platters are transformative – but it's a case of when to decant and when not to. A sauce in a jug is instantly more delicious than a sauce in a saucepan, but a stew in a cold white dish can look like it came from the chilled aisle at the supermarket.

There are things gathering dust in everyone's house that can be fashioned into pretty vessels on a supper table. From old tiles to baskets, there are many objects of beauty just waiting to be repurposed. Slabs of slate or roof shingles can be treated with a coating of mineral oil and used for serving butter, charcuterie or cheese. Put your wine bottles in a metal bucket filled with ice. Use off-cuts of wood as placemats, and chopping boards to serve food – a deconstructed salad, perhaps, of broken-off leaves of little gem lettuces, alongside a small jug of creamy dressing, or radishes with their leaves still on, with a small dish of salt and a plate of butter. From eggcups to finger bowls, tin teapots to glass bottles, no vessel is too small, large or odd-shaped not to be of use for something.

Knives, Forks and Spoons

Cutlery has always been man's attempt to improve upon the perfect tools we were born with: our sharp teeth for cutting and our smooth hands for scooping and pronging. Many of us in the world continue to use our hands to eat because they're simply brilliant at the job. There's no better equipment for eating corn on the cob, or ribs, or lobster, or fruit or toast. In fact, I'm often tempted to do away with cutlery altogether and just get stuck in with my fingers. Cutlery as we know it – from knives and forks to chopsticks – has formalised the way we eat, removing that deeply connected relationship we would have otherwise had with the texture and feel of our food.

Over many hundreds of years, the Western world has gradually formed the trinity of knife, fork and spoon, each taking particular charge of a role in getting food from plate to mouth. From the first fragments of flint, selected and shaped to sit in the hand, we have tried to finesse the function of eating, to make it less servile, less liable to dribble down our fronts. The history of cutlery can broadly be seen as one of a gradual blunting and de-sharpening, of thoughts to possible injury and health and safety, so that over the centuries table knives became more suitable for butter spreading than tearing apart a beast.

By the 19th Century, formal cutlery was firmly established in Western psyche. Mrs Beeton's books illustrated complete sets of cutlery that proliferated out from the centrum of our plates in an array of shapes and sizes – each one suited to the elaborate requirements of fiddly Victorian courses. Since then, fortunately, we have rationalised our table equipment somewhat, and today few of us would go beyond stocking one size of knife, fork and a couple of different sizes of spoon in our cutlery drawer.

Knives

Although every other aspect of our kitchens is virtually unrecognisable from
its equivalent hundreds of years ago, knives have hardly changed in concept
since medieval times. It is not possible to imagine eating meat without a sharp
cutting instrument, but the knives we set on our tables today are a much
tamer version of the vicious, double-edged blades used by our ancestors
– for both feeding and fighting. The first metal knives were cast in copper,
and then bronze, and then iron. Medieval illustrations show men carrying a
personal cache of cutlery about their person: a knife worn on a belt (ready to
be used for lunch or in self-defence) and a spoon tucked in hats or jackets.
In the 16th Century, eating knives became very long, thin and elegant; the
handles given ornate decorative treatment in carved ivory or wood with jet,
ebony and coloured bone used in inlays. By the 19th Century, handles were
as varied as the market demanded, but as supplies of bone, ivory and antler
horn diminished, a more sustainable replacement had to be found. Celluloid,
invented in 1869, was a thermoplastic that could be made to look and feel
like ivory at a fraction of the price.

Forks

The ancient Greeks and Romans used two-pronged forks to help them steady the meat they were carving. However the fork as a piece of eating – rather than serving – equipment, is a relative newcomer to the table, and was traditionally viewed as a rather effeminate implement – a little bit fey, not very manly. In the late 11th Century, small eating forks began to appear in Venice, spreading through Italy after being introduced by a Byzantine princess. Thomas Beckett brought this new trend back to England after his exile in Italy and, according to legend, he tried to sell the idea to Henry II on the basis that forks could, handily, be washed. Henry II replied, indignant: "But so can your hands". Clergymen also condemned their use, arguing that only human fingers, created by God, should touch His provisions. It wasn't until the 1670s that the fork began to achieve general popularity, and by the early 19th Century, four pronged forks were being made in England, with Sheffield becoming the international centre of the cutlery industry.

Spoons

Every race on earth has fashioned a spoon for itself, out of whatever they had to hand, from seashells to horn: they are the most elemental design in the cutlery drawer. The first spoons were carved from wood, and the word spoon comes from the Anglo-Saxon 'spon' which means 'chip'. They were flattish and shallow – perfect for coarse stews scooped from a cauldron. In the second half of the 15th Century, spoons changed shape to the way we know them today – long and thin, with deep bowls – so that men and women sporting large, stiff-laced ruff collars could avoid soup dribbling.

These days, to ask for a spoon is seen to be a rather infantile request, spoon-feeding bringing to mind babies or elderly people with no teeth, but I love eating with a spoon. We eat with spoons when we eat alone, when we feast on leftovers standing by the fridge, but why should spoon-feeding be the preserve of solitary feasts and stolen mouthfuls? Spoons are so comforting, so simple and rudimentary, we should use them more. Risotto is delicious from a spoon, as is fish pie and peas, and I wouldn't want to tackle a bowl of spaghetti without a spoon to help me twirl it.

Materials

Silver

Though high maintenance and expensive, silver adds something soulful
to a table that stainless steel can never match. It's easy to spot silver – the
warmth of the metal and the weight of it in your hand is unmistakable. High-
grade European silver will have the mark 925 engraved on it, indicating the
percentage (92.5 per cent) of pure silver required to qualify as sterling (the
remaining 7.5 per cent will be copper). It's a delicate material – it scratches
easily and will tarnish on contact with acids such as lemon, salt and eggs, so
you must polish it regularly if you don't want it to look dark and dappled (see
right), and it must never see the inside of a dishwasher. But sterling silver
loves to be used. The more you eat with it, the more beautiful it will become.
Exposure to the air will give silver a patina – a lustrous, mellow finish. I think
even dirty silver looks quite special, on a vase or candle stick, say. Water-
damaged silver looks lovely at a table, especially on white linen, but it's best
to avoid very corroded silver – steer clear of pieces that have very dark brown,
black or purple-blue tones on them.

Silver plate

A turning point for everyday cutlery was the invention of silver-plating by electrolysis, patented in 1840 by the Birmingham company Elkington. Silver-plating is nickel, copper or zinc which has had a layer of pure silver deposited on it to give a silver finish. The thickness of the plate is key: a generous deposit of 35 microns of silver will probably last 35 to 50 years, but cutlery (or anything, for that matter) that calls itself 'silver plate' can be incredibly thinly coated – a dusting really – as little as three microns of silver. Whatever the thickness, the 'plate' will inevitably wear off over time, so always buy pieces that feel heavy – the heavier the better.

Stainless steel

Stainless steel, invented by Harry Breaerley in 1914 in Sheffield, changed the look and feel of cutlery forever. Made from a mixture of chromium, iron and nickel, stainless steel meant that affordable (non-silver) cutlery, for the first time, could be made in one piece – rather than a metal end with a wooden, bone or ceramic handle. Before then, looking after knives and forks would mean a long battle against rust and corrosion, necessitating hours of elbow-grease, but this new material paved the way for the dishwasher-safe-packed cutlery drawers we have today: sturdy, practical and standing up to millions of hot washes without a single blemish. When buying it you should look for markings that read 18/8 or 18/10 (percentages of chromium and nickel) – the higher the number the better. Unmarked may be of lesser quality.

How to clean silver

Tarnished silver can be restored with Silver Dip. Sponge it over the knife or fork until the tarnish is removed. Rinse it in a separate bowl of hot water and dry it off. Next, apply polish with a foam rubber sponge. Allow to dry. Then, brush off the dry powder with a cloth.

Buying cutlery second-hand

Thanks to the modern preference for stainless steel, coupled with the Victorian and Edwardian fashion for myriad knives and forks at each place setting, high-grade antique cutlery is plentiful and inexpensive. Look for it in out-of-town antique shops and house clearances, bound together in incomplete sets with elastic bands. Check each knife for sharpness and ensure it's properly weighted (heavier handles are best) and that the staining and patina on the blades or tines is not too heavy. A good table knife falls slightly heavily in your palm, is correctly weighted for slicing and has a good, sharp blade. A fork should be lighter, more delicate, and not too big or too sharp. Cutlery looks brilliant mismatched – don't feel you should buy an entire service at once. The splendour of old things is that they aren't perfect, and anyway, you'll notice the beauty of it more if each piece is slightly different.

Keep an eye out for the unusual. Solid bone spoons work beautifully with chocolate and dark puddings and won't corrode, so they're particularly perfect for boiled eggs. Small wooden spoons are good with dry things – salt, spices and so on. Little enamel spoons are very pretty and can come in jewel colours: perfect for use as coffee spoons.

Look for knives with interesting handles. They can elevate an ordinary knife to a thing of real beauty. Search for one-off pieces in amber, horn, mother-of-pearl, glass or ceramic. Pewter is a hardened tin with a blue-ish tint. It gets a soft grey patina over time, and is pliable so must be hand washed. Wood can be beautiful, but must also be washed carefully and dried before you store it.

Where to put them

When it comes to knives, forks and spoons there is, of course, a 'right' way to lay them on the table. The concentration of cutlery and glassware to the right-hand side of the plate is thought to have originated in France, with the idea that you hold your napkin with your left hand and eat with your right. Conventions decree that the fork should be held in the left hand (it, conveniently, has four letters, as does 'left'), and the knife be held the right (which has five letters, as does right; incidentally 'glass' and 'spoon' also have five letters, which means they should be on the right, too). But on your table, don't be bound by convention. Wrap your knife and fork in your napkin if you want; put them horizontally at the top of your plate; put all the cutlery in a big tin at the centre of the table, if you fancy, or do away with knives and forks all together and just offer spoons. Butlers in grand houses may have to adhere to rigid rules, but in your own home, do what you like. Some like to lay the pudding spoons across the top of each setting, but I always think it looks cluttered and all too often they have dollops of shepherd's pie on them by the time you get to crumble. Instead, bring pudding spoons to the table with the pudding – in a jug, like a bunch of tulips.

You can use whatever knife and fork shape you like on your table, but cutlery – or flatware, as it's called in America – is generally available in three sizes: 'luncheon', 'place' and 'dinner'. Dinner knives and forks are about eight centimetres longer than 'place' sizes, while the 'luncheon' size is about one centimetre smaller than 'place'.

Serving tools

Generally speaking, I think letting people prod and scoop food from dishes with their own forks is preferable to providing a full kit of intimidating tongs and serving spoons. However, some dishes lend themselves more easily to this than others. Bringing a steaming pot of stew to a table before doling it out onto plates is comforting and homely – a big, tin ladle is the most generous and useful serving spoon. A bowl of green salad never feels quite right unless it's pincered onto your plate with a set of wooden salad servers – but two wooden spoons would do the trick if you don't have a set. For everything else – peas, sauces, potatoes – oversized spoons or normal cutlery are perfect.

Cutlery Shapes

Knives	Forks

Knives

Steak knife
Serated blade. Good for
crusty bread.

Pudding knife
Curved handle. Intended for
more cut-able puddings like
tarts, or for peeling figs.

Fish knife
Pointed end.

Butter knife
Flat and blunt.

Tea knife
Small. Perfect on a
breakfast tray, a butter dish
or on a picnic.

Forks

Fruit fork
Two tines.

Pastry fork
Thick left tine.

Oyster fork
Three wide tines. Also known as
a cocktail fork.

Fish fork
Thick outer tines.

Spoons

Cream soup spoon
A round bowl specially designed to
dip into cream soup bowls.

Bouillon spoon
Soup spoon, smaller than the cream
soup spoon.

Trifle spoon
Shell shaped.

Fruit spoon
Short and round.

Grapefruit spoon
Serated edge and/or a sharply
pointed end.

Salt spoon
Miniature, traditionally used in gold
cellars (salt corrodes silver).

Demitasse
A tiny spoon intended for coffee.

Glasses and Coffee Cups

We've been using cups for drinking for millennia, from goblets to chalices made in all manner of materials from skulls to clay, wood and metal, but drinking vessels haven't always been part of the table placement. In the 15th Century, at banquets, glasses were regularly kept on a separate table; a servant would bring you a drink every time you wanted one.

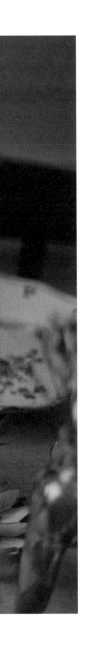

Modern wine glasses – with their elegant, flower-like stems and bulbs – have provided a sense of occasion to washing down your supper since at least the 14th Century, when the glassblowers of Venice perfected a shape that would drink well, show off the wine and look beautiful, too. Glasses continue to be the jewels of the table, reflecting candlelight and adding to the special ambience.

Fine lead crystal glassware used to be extremely rare – only made by the expert glassmakers in Murano, Italy. But by the early 20th Century, the techniques had caught on and were copied, and fine glassware became more readily available. The Victorians relished having special glasses for different purposes: sherry, white wine, brandy, port and so on – all highly wrought and hand etched. But in the modern era we have veered towards clean lines: clear, simple, practical glassware that is streamlined and practical – and we have also gone supersize.

I loathe the fashion for enormous balloon-like wine glasses that carry a pint of wine. If nothing else, they don't fit in the dishwasher and invariably get smashed in the washing up bowl. When it comes to glasses, small is perfect. Cut-glass Edwardian sherry glasses are lovely for wine and look great mismatched, so you can collect them individually from antique shops. Low tumblers or goblets with heavy, stubby stems are ideal for wine or water. As with every aspect of laying the table, there is an etiquette for glassware (big for white wine, bigger for red wine) but I think it's chic to serve red wine in a sherry glass; water in a jam jar or Morroccan tea glass, and coffee or ice cream in a tumbler. You shouldn't feel at all restricted by what you pour into which. Whatever looks nice, and feels right, is correct.

Buying glass second-hand

If you are picking up glasses from house clearances, charity shops or antique fairs, it pays to know the difference in quality.

Fine glassware

Lead crystal is the finest of all glassware. Made with lead or a similar chemical at a very high temperature and often mouth-blown, etched or engraved, it is thin and delicate and will chime with a high 'ding' when you tap it. The glass must be at least 24 per cent lead to carry the lead crystal appellation; the lead gives it more weight, increases its resilience and gives it more sparkle – reflecting a rainbow of colours when polished. There will be a brilliance and clarity to it when you hold it to the light. Good crystalware will also balance well on the table, as it will be properly weighted in the base. Look at the rim of the glass. Rolled rims are cheaper and more durable; cut rims are more delicate and fine looking – you'll see them on handmade glass and very fine crystal. Cut rims involve the edge of the glass being reheated until it is semi-molten, whereupon the excess glass is cut away, leaving a soft-looking finish.

Mercury glass is mirrored and looks magical on a table; Opaline glass originated in France in the 19th Century and is cloudy, almost milky looking. Bristol Blue glass was created in the West of England in the 18th Century, and is an inky, Yves-Klein blue, which makes beautiful small vases for white flowers. Two of the Bristol factories that made it were resurrected in the 1980s, and you can find plentiful copies in chain stores.

Everyday glassware

Cheaper glassware is made with 'soda lime' a combination of limestone, silica and other materials. It is more durable and can withstand a bit of bashing about. It can also be tempered (as the classic Duralex tumblers are) so you can use them for hot things, and to cook with. Soda lime glass will be pressed into moulds, rather than mouth-blown. Recycled glass will have bubbles and imperfections and is always heavier and, more often than not, will be tinted or coloured as clarity is impossible with the process of recycling.

Shapes of glass

Sherry and cordial glasses
The prettiest glasses on
a table; small, shapely,
light, perfectly formed and
collectable.

Red and white wine glasses
Come in all shapes and
sizes. Traditionally red wine
glasses are bigger than
white wine glasses because
the larger the bowl the
better the oxidisation (and
therefore development of
flavours). Red burgundy
glasses are the biggest of all.

Morroccan tea glass
Traditionally used for
drinking Mahgreb mint
leaf tea, they come in
beautiful patterns and
colours and can be used
for anything.

Tumbler
Footless and stubby. Ideal
for water, but also lovely for
wine. Small tumblers make
perfect pots for mousse or
custardy puddings.

Champagne flutes
Tall and thin, so the
bubbles don't escape.
But I think Champagne
is most delicious drunk
from Champagne saucers
– low, shallow glasses with
delicate stems.

Coffee cups, teacups and saucers

No supper feels quite complete without a tray of strong coffee. Dark and
really intensely coloured things – chocolate, inky-black coffee, sweets
wrapped in metallic paper – feel so luxurious; a kind of midnight treat.
Think about contrasts after your pudding has been cleared away. I always
bring coffee in on a tray, even though I'm only carting it from kettle to
kitchen table – because it looks so special that way, jostled together cups,
miniature teaspoons, a small jug of milk and bowl of soft brown sugar or
jagged sugar lumps alongside. For after-supper coffee cups, hunt down the
smallest, smallest you can find. Literally child-sized, with a saucer or without.
Again, these can be mismatched, so buy them when you see them – they're
called demitasse (which means half a cup). Make an Italian stove-top pot of
espresso coffee and serve it in small doses.

It's also lovely to offer a teapot with fresh mint leaves steeped in boiling water for people who don't fancy caffeine, but serve it short, in a teacup, not in great gallon-sized mugs. Mugs, I think, are really best at teatime, with proper tea in them and a biscuit.

Teacups with saucers can either be footed or flat – standing upright in their saucer or sitting snugly in it. For after-dinner tea drinkers, the finer the cup the better – look for single bone china teacups in junk shops and mismatch your set.

Flowers and Lighting

Flowers are the greatest source of joy for those of us who like to set the table. They bring colour in a way nothing else can. With flowers you mark the time of year: spring bulbs at your Easter table, hips and haws in autumn; fir cones and mistletoe at Christmas. But gathering a bunch of flowers for the table is a relatively new trend. Until the 19th Century, fresh flowers were seen as being too rustic, and so silk and feathers would adorn tabletops. By the start of the 20th Century real flowers made up for lost time, and tables were piled with ever more elaborate floral displays. In grand houses, the foreman gardener would be in charge of arranging the flowers in silver bowls. Flowers make food look better – more wholesome – because they remind you of what grows naturally in the earth. Which is why a little egg cup of daisies will make even a slice of leftover pizza look quite special.

Whatever the time of year, when it comes to putting flowers on your table, lose the idea of flower arranging. Flowers should always look fresh and spontaneous, never overworked or designed. They should look like they've come straight from the garden: sunkissed, dewy or frosty, rambling and natural. Always buy more flowers than you think you need – I know that sounds extravagant, but abundance is what you're after, and when you strip them back (which you always should) you'll be left with a lot less than you started with. Having said that, you can make a single bunch of petrol-station carnations or chrysanthemums go really far if you separate the blooms into single, open heads and pop them into individual glasses.

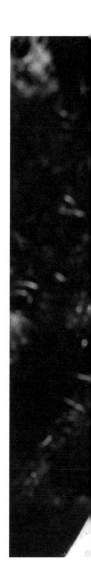

If you can't find any nice flowers, gather bunches of herbs: a posy of mint, for example, suits a tin jug. Terracotta potted bulbs from the garden centre look charming lined up the centre of a table – even the plastic potted herbs you get in the supermarket can look lovely wrapped in a jacket of newspaper, and tied with brown string. Wherever you live there will be something you can put in a vase on the table. Prune a few russetty leaves from a tree for a simple autumnal display; place a branch of pine cones down the centre of the table, or line up a few tubs of potted lavender. Even picked nettles (wear rubber gloves) make a romantic, scruffy little bunch in a tiny painted jug. Anything wild will look beautiful no matter what you do with it. Rosehips in September are my favourite. Sheaves of wheat, so popular in the elaborate table displays of the 1980s, can look modern if they are the only flowers on your table and are tied in a low bunch with brown string. Sprigs of motorway-layby blackberries, crab-apples or blackcurrants, branches with silvery leaves, even a whole bunch of rhubarb, leaves attached, can look pretty. If all else fails, a bunch of supermarket rosemary in a small glass (with no water) will work. There will be something growing on your street, in your park, or for sale in your supermarket – something somewhere that will bring the beauty of nature to your supper table.

Rules of picking wildflowers

It is against the law to pick flowers without permission, and parks and public spaces with lovely rose gardens or daffodils would obviously be against you taking snips. There are also plants that are protected because they are endangered – these are on the Botanical Society of Great Britain's website and include ladies' slipper orchids, adder's tongue and threadmoss – and many other traditional British wildflowers that are being inched out by pollution and aggressive farming. If a single type of flower is growing abundantly on a roadside verge, though, it's unlikely to cause problems if you pick one or two – and some farmers might thank you for pruning some of their weeds, but be aware it's basically stealing. Ask permission and don't be greedy.

daisy

forget-me-not

mallow

scabious

lesser celandine

wild rose

Buying flowers

Not all of us can get to Covent Garden flower market at 4am and really good
local florists are, sadly, thin on the ground these days. The truth is most of
us will buy our flowers at the supermarket. But be your own florist. Work
your magic with them. The first thing to do at any flower stand is look in the
bucket the flowers are kept in – there should be fresh, clean water in there;
you don't want parched, traumatised flowers. Next, look for tight blooms –
no sagging or limpness. Roses and peonies should be bought about two days
before you need them so they have time to open out, but try and buy other
flowers on the day you want them, so you can guarantee they'll look their

best. Next, check the base of the stem – it should be tight, clean and freshly cut – and make sure the leaves are firm and bright green.

Readymade bouquets always feature things I hate amongst a few mean stems of ranunculus, like waxy ferns or grasses dyed purple. It's much cheaper to buy single types of flowers, which you can then group as you please. If you're nervous of colour, go for a romantic all white palette – or all yellow, choosing three types of flower in the same colour. Pink and white always looks lovely together, as do shades of purple and blue, whilst pink, orange and red together looks fresh and modern. Reject the mass-produced foliage you get in supermarket bouquets, and mix your own greenery in in the shape of mint, rosemary or flowering chives, bought in the main shopping aisles. Think about texture and composition, but don't overthink it.

As soon as you get home, take all the wrapping off, snip the plastic band that binds them and splay the flowers out on your table. Before you do anything, cut an inch off the bottom of each stalk and give them a long drink in the sink.

Displaying

Don't think of flowers as the centrepiece – a huge vase that dominates the middle of the table; they should be accents. On a table at which you eat and talk, flowers must be low – well below eye level – which means vases must be no more that a few inches tall, unless, that is, you are sectioning off part of your bigger table for a smaller gathering, in which case a large, loosely sprawling bunch of roses or branches in a lusterware vase or a hurricane shade looks wonderful. In general, though, avoid big vases. They seem to make even a lot of expensive flowers seem rather mean, wherever you put them, and can be a huge obstacle for chat. No one should have to duck around flowers in order to see the person opposite them, so always be on the hunt for really miniature containers – egg cups, Christening cups, teacups, sugar bowls, pretty tin cans and so on. So many forgotten objects make great flower holders – they just have to be watertight. Glass and crystal suit all flowers and will add a sparkle to a candlelit table. Gather vases together in little groups, bearing in mind the 'Rule of Three': odd numbers are always more pleasing than even. Think in groups of varying heights, too: three types

of blue flower, for example, in three shades of blue, in three different jugs. Or three bunches of three types of roses in three different pale pinks. The benefit of clusters of flowers is that they look good from every angle, so there will be something lovely to look at from every seat at your table.

Match the flowers with a vase – shiny, silver or mirrored vases look perfect filled with pink peonies, sweet peas, lavender and rosemary. Hyacinths look right in tin buckets; scented herbs call for weathered pots; rusty watering cans beg to be filled generously with daffodils, and old-fashioned roses look right in faded painted jugs. But don't be afraid to experiment with the less conventional. Contrast your colours – vivid red geraniums look amazing in a green malachite vase. Try putting something very elegant, like a rose, in an earthenware pot, or something wild in a very ornate vase – flowering kale can look great in a solid silver jug.

Arranging

Supermarket flowers can be absolutely transformed by cutting them low: frighteningly low, so that you feel you're ruining them, and so that they rest on the lip of the vase. Stalks should be cut sharply on an angle, and scrupulously stripped of all leaves that fall below the waterline (this will be all but one of two of the leaves, probably). This feels incredibly wasteful, as you'll end up throwing away almost all the stalk and greenery, but it really is the way to make supermarket blooms look their absolute best, and it's what florists do.

Lighting

Since the human race began we have gathered round flames to eat, and so the flicker of fire will always be symbolic of gathering together. Anyone who knows the pleasures of the table loves the cosy, twinkly glow of candlelight; overhead lamps and pendants are the enemy of an intimate supper. Candles will only last the length of a wick – they are not reusable and so they are a luxury, a once-only thing, destined to come to an end. In our world of instant lighting and the ubiquitous glow of mobile phones, candlelight is special. Now they are no longer a necessity in ordinary life, they are a marking ritual, casting a flattering light over china and glass, food and faces.

I like a table that is really dark and twinkly, lit entirely by candles. The benefit, too, is that you will plunge the unwashed pans in the sink into darkness. If you're worried about the room being too dark, put a collection of candles on a mirrored tray on the table. It will softly reflect and amplify the light. Napoleonic tables had a similar thing called a *place surtout* – a mirrored platform in the centre of the table to pool and reflect the candlelight. It's subtle but magical.

Never have scented candles anywhere near food or your kitchen, and certainly not on the table. Look, instead, for long coloured tapers (I love orange and pink), curled beeswax ones or short, stubby church candles.

The ideal candleholders are short – ten or 12 centimetres – so that the candles cast their light wide and low. Flickering wicks at eye level are distracting. I find tealights tinny and cheap looking on their own. However, when placed in lanterns and hung from trees in outdoor gatherings, they can be enchanting. To make a jam-jar lantern, simply wind garden wire tightly around the rim of a jar and hang it. To make a tin can lantern, steam the label off a tin can and puncture lots of holes in it before dropping a tea light in.

Wind foliage around candlesticks to make a garland or group church candles in uneven numbers and uneven heights; tall, medium and low, or plant tapers in terracotta pots filled with moss. Wrap candles in foil and put them in the fridge for two hours before lighting them – they'll burn slower and more evenly.

Feast

A truly welcoming table has something edible already on it when everyone sits down – a promise of what's to come. Bring your main course to the table to a drum roll by all means – but set the scene for it with delicious things that can be tucked into right now: a warm loaf of bread wrapped in a clean cloth, a plate of flavoured butter, a bowl of minted yoghurt, perhaps some bright yellow aioli or emerald salsa verde – something spoonable that will match the feast. It's extra washing up, but I love decanting condiments on the table – into pretty bowls, or, with mustards and relishes, into a glass tumbler or ceramic pot, with a small silver or wooden spoon. Top, top quality olive oil is a delicious accompaniment to most things and can be decanted into cheap tin teapots, which looks superb and is perfect for drizzling on risotto. Even a jagged hunk of parmesan on a wooden board, with a grater alongside, will make the table look more tempting.

Salt

However marvellously seasoned your cooking is, there is no excuse for omitting salt and pepper cellars from your table. Salt is a delicious, treaty thing that has graced our supper tables since the 6th Century, and a table is incomplete with it. Salt does extraordinary things to food, and as such, throughout history it has been treated with respect. Indeed, the phrase to be 'worth your salt' derives from its importance: in medieval times the salt cellar would be placed strategically on the table, before the place setting of the most honoured guest or lord of the house. To be able to reach it to season your food was a mark of achievement. You were being told you were very special.

Some people like their food very, very salty, and a cook shouldn't be offended if their guests want a toothsome crunch on their broccoli. Tastes vary, and it's silly to take it personally when people blacken with pepper the soup you have agonised over getting right. Because chefs can be precious about their guests seasoning their food, people feel embarrassed about craving a little salt or pepper, so I prefer to omit mills and grinders altogether. Grinding makes seasoning ostentatious. Offer generous pinch bowls instead – of ground pepper and flaky sea salt, perhaps with a small enamel or wooden spoon. Scallop shells are brilliant, but a small saucer or egg cup would be perfect, too.

Flavoured salts

Mix crushed fennel seeds, finely chopped rosemary or crushed chilli flakes
with a good flaky sea salt for a delicious savoury sprinkle. You can also buy
beautiful coloured salts – seaweed salt or pink Himalayan salt looks so pretty
in a small glass dish. If you're making a curry, put out a dish of mixed salt –
white pepper, cumin seeds, fennel seeds, garam masala and chilli flakes – for
scattering on top.

Water

Eating without water to hand makes me panicky. The catch of serving lots of delicious salty, fatty, buttery food is that your guests will soon be parched, and for the same reason I always provide plenty of salt on the table (and don't take offense when people use it), I don't want to force people to apologisingly plead for a glass of water. All tables should be set generously with jugs or bottles of water, with a separate glass in which to drink it. However civilised it is to wash your supper down with delicate sips of wine, sometimes you just want to glug and glug and for that, only water will do. It's fancy to have bottled water, but what's wrong with the stuff out of the tap? It's what I always serve. I'm very anti iced water with food. I find it jarring to have something incredibly cold alongside warm things, not to mention the fiddle of trying to pour a small glass of water from a jug filled with a million ice cubes. Room temperature water is hugely underrated. It's much more refreshing for the very thirsty – you can actually swig it – it fits with all wine and food, and there is an endless source of it right there at the sink. Offer your water in a large jug or carafe and put two or three on the table if you have lots of people – everyone should be able to reach it.

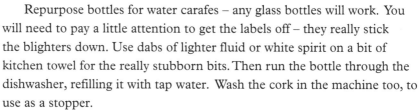

Repurpose bottles for water carafes – any glass bottles will work. You will need to pay a little attention to get the labels off – they really stick the blighters down. Use dabs of lighter fluid or white spirit on a bit of kitchen towel for the really stubborn bits. Then run the bottle through the dishwasher, refilling it with tap water. Wash the cork in the machine too, to use as a stopper.

Flavoured water can be delicious; the key is to slightly overdo it with volume of flavourings. Fill a whole jug with halved (rather than sliced) limes, lemons or oranges and top up with water. Chunky bits of cucumber look good too, or whole bunches of mint – great posies of it that fill the entire jug.

If you do like iced water (as many do), there are some things you can do to make it special. Drop single edible flowers and leaves into your ice cube tray when you're filling it – look for borage, chive blossoms, violets, marigolds, lemon verbena, lemon balm, mint and nasturtiums.

Bread

My French step-father could not conceive of a meal without bread, yet I know so many women of my generation who recoil in horror at the idea of eating it, thinking of the bread basket in restaurants as the nexus of exercising the fiercest will power. Yes, it very well might make me fat, but I know I could never sacrifice it. Bread is the centrepiece of any good table. It is the grounding force of any supper, small or large. Bread is comforting like no other food, and can miraculously transform even the most humble offering into a feast. Bread has remained, throughout the ages, as Margaret Visser puts it in her wonderful book *The Rituals of Dinner*, "a deeply significant symbol, a substance honoured and sacred." A loaf is the ultimate sharing food, and to break it is, as we know, to offer friendship.

If you have space, I love a whole loaf (unsliced and warmed in the oven) on a bread board, with a bread knife. Or thickly slice or tear it and put it in a wicker basket lined with a generous napkin, tucking in some ramekins of butter. An upturned Panama hat makes a sweet bread basket, too. You can also make an informal one out of a brown paper bag, cut and folded down into a bowl shape. If you have less space, swaddle your warm bread in a clean dishcloth. I never lay side plates for bread – use the table, or your supper plate.

Not only do we eat less bread than we ever did, but the bread we do eat is factory-made, gum-and-stabiliser-pumped plastic. It is incredibly easy – not to mention deeply satisfying – to make your own.

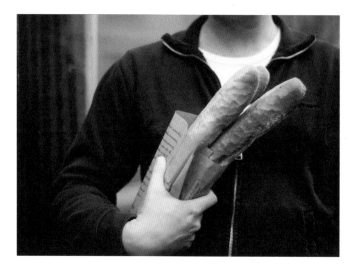

Soda bread

Since Tudor times, when bread-ovens became popular in home kitchens, the smell of a baking has been synonymous with a welcoming table. Even if the supper you serve is just plates of shop-bought cheeses and some cobbled together salads, a homemade loaf – warm from the oven – will fill the room with the promise of good things. This recipe is brilliant because you can have a warm loaf of bread on the table within the hour; no kneading, no rising, no fuss.

250g strong wholemeal bread flour
10g baking powder
1tsp salt
35g butter at room temperature
15ml cider vinegar
60ml whole milk
75ml semi-skimmed milk
1 egg, beaten

Pour the whole milk into a jug, tip in the vinegar, stir once and leave to sit for ten minutes to thicken. In a separate bowl, sift the flour, baking powder and salt together and work in the butter, rubbing it with your fingers until it disappears. Add the vinegar/milk mix and all the other ingredients and mix with your hands. Add a scattering of flour if it's too sticky. Shape into a flattish disc, score across the top in a cross shape, dust with more flour and let it rest for 20 minutes. Put in a really hot (200°C) oven for half an hour. Serve immediately – it really doesn't keep longer than a day.

Butter

The French may disapprove – but for me, where there is bread, there must
be butter. Along with salt, lemons and good olive oil, butter makes everything
delicious, and a pat of it lends itself easily to looking beautiful. Take it out
of the foil and put it on a small plate, with a little knife alongside. Or scoop
some butter onto small squares of slate, or onto terracotta or Morrocan tiles.

Flavoured butter

It may well be gilding the lily, but there are lots of lovely tricks you can
do to butter to make it even more delicious. For something very subtly
sophisticated, salt your butter at home. Turn some top quality flaky salt into
some good, unsalted, room temperature butter. Then refrigerate. It makes
for an incredibly moreish crunch. A horseradish butter will make plain corn
on the cob or green beans sing: mix butter with a teaspoon of mustard and a
teaspoon of grated horseradish, and season with black pepper.

Mels's bagna caudo

My friend Mels served her easy version of this salty, anchovy-laced butter with bread when we had supper on her roof, and it was easily one of the most delicious things I've ever eaten. If you insist on serving a starter, make a bowl of this with warm bread and crudité. Blitz a tin of drained anchovies with a pat of butter, the juice of a lemon, two garlic cloves and a generous few grinds of black pepper with a food processor, until smooth and spreadable. Add more lemon juice if you want a thinner consistency.

Summer sauce

A herby, garlicky sauce goes with almost everything, particularly roast chicken or roast fish, and any green veg. It's sublime with grilled or barbequed lamb. Make it with whatever soft, green herbs you can get your hands on and taste it to get the balance right. Blitz together a mix of parsley, mint, dill, tarragon and coriander with a scattering of capers, a few tinned anchovy fillets, a clove of garlic, and the juice of half a lemon. Pour in a stream of very good olive oil until it's spoonable.

Aioli

This is particularly good with poached chicken and boiled vegetables.

Peel three garlic cloves and pound together with a pinch of salt. In a bowl, drop a single egg yolk, a teaspoon of water and half the garlic and whisk together. Drizzle some really good olive oil in, very slowly, in a single stream, whisking as you go. It will thicken and lighten in colour. Stop adding oil when you get a nice, thick, gloopy sauce. If it gets too thick, add a few drops of water. Taste, salt and add the rest of the garlic if you feel it needs it. Let it sit for an hour or so in the fridge before serving (but do eat it that day).

Harissa

My version of this Moroccan sauce is not orthodox, but it's utterly delicious with lamb or burgers. Think of it as a sophisticated homemade ketchup. Blend a drained jar of peeled, cored, deseeded red peppers with a teaspoon of caraway seeds, a teaspoon of ground cumin, three garlic cloves, lots of sea salt and black pepper and drizzle in good olive oil until it's a spoonable consistency. Add chilli if you want it spicy.

Minted yoghurt

I love this with roast lamb, but it's good with couscous and vegetarian recipes too. Roughly chop a large bunch of mint, crush a garlic clove and stir them into natural yoghurt. Add a swirl of really good olive oil.

Basil oil

This vibrant green sauce is delicious with salads – tomato and mozzarella, obviously – but also so good with cold roast beef. In a food processor, whiz two large bunches of basil and a clove of garlic, before adding some good olive oil in a slow stream. Season with salt and pepper.

Acknowledgements

Thanks, first, to my collaborator and friend Charlotte Bland, whose soulful photographs, humour, energy and style gave life to this book. Thanks also to Ziggy Hanaor, the most calm and supportive editor, and to Lydia Starkey for her beautiful illustrations. Thank you to Ewan from The Lacquer Chest for his belief in the project from the start, and to the many friends and family who so generously gave me their ideas, houses and hands, particularly to Matthew Blay, Oliver Guy and Emma Ziegler; Alice Blacker and Owen Gundry, Otto and Winifred; and Reuben Thomas and Vix McCarthy. Thank you to my mother in law, Camilla Thomas, whose eye for fabrics and china has been a huge inspiration, and to my amazingly talented and supportive mum, Sarah Shuckburgh, who can make a table look beautiful better than anyone I know. Love and thanks also to my family: my beautiful baby boy Adair; Amy, Jeremy, Clementine, Dotty, Al, Kalli, and my darling dad. Finally, this book is dedicated to my husband, Archie Thomas, without whom nothing would be possible.

Published by Cicada Books Limited

Written by Hannah Shuckburgh
Photography by Charlotte Bland
Illustrations by Lydia Starkey
Edited by Ziggy Hanaor
Designed by Lisa Sjukur for April

British Library Cataloguing-in-Publication Data.

A CIP record for this book is available from the British Library.
ISBN: 978-1-908714-04-6

© 2013 Cicada Books Limited

Cicada Books Limited
48 Burghley Road
London NW5 1UE
United Kingdom

T +44 207 209 2259
E ziggy@cicadabooks.co.uk
W www.cicadabooks.co.uk

Printed in China